smorgasborgman
by
JIMBORGMAN

with an introduction by Jerry Springer

text and design by Lynn Goodwin Borgman

Armadillo Press

Published by

ARMADILLO PRESS
P.O. Box 8812
Cincinnati, Ohio 45208

Library of Congress Catalogue Card Number **82-73352**
ISBN **0-9609632-0-0**

The contents of this book originally appeared in the *Cincinnati Enquirer,* ©1979, 1980, 1981, 1982.
Jim Borgman's cartoons are distributed exclusively by *King Features Syndicate.*

Printed in Cincinnati, Ohio by *The Merten Company.* Ⓜ

Typography by *Pagemakers.*

To Mom and Dad

THANKS FOR SPECIAL HELP to: Rich West, Stephen Mautner, Jerry Becker, Thom Gephardt, Bill Keating, Bob Temmen, Bob Ratterman, Joanne Maly, Tom and Mary Borgman, Betty Woods Balter, Virlea Woods, Mike and Marian Peters, Jan and Duane Powell, Ken Corbus, Mike Molinelli, Linda Parker, Susan Crain, the Merten folks and Marian Borgman, my special assistant; and all the many other people who have lent advice and support.

I WOULD ALSO like to acknowledge and thank these people from whose work I have learned the most: Ronald Searle, Pat Oliphant, Jeff MacNelly, Walt Kelly, Honore Daumier, George Herriman, Bruce Springsteen, Ellen Goodman, David Broder, Mike Peters, Mort Drucker, Saul Steinberg, Mike Keefe, Heinrich Kley, Joan Didion, Edward Sorel, Tony Auth and the people at National Public Radio.

Introduction

Tough luck. This is my chance to get even and I can't draw. I, on behalf of all of us who have been victimized over the years by Jim Borgman's outrageous pen, have been asked to introduce this collection of visions – the world according to Borgman.

I don't like him. First of all, he's smart. Never did like smart kids. You know the type. Glasses – carried a briefcase to school – always did his homework. He was never one of the guys. While we were playing ball or salivating over Annette Funicello, he was drawing her ears (he would later learn to keep his eye on the ball).

Second reason I don't like him is the way he draws me. To him I'm nothing but a nose. Well, he should pick on something else. He's no beaut himself. When he was a kid, he was so ugly his Mom used to go everywhere with him just so she wouldn't have to kiss him good-bye.

And then I don't like him because he's going to make all the money on this book. The best I'm going to get is a free copy, and not even that unless I say something nice. Well, I can't do that, but perhaps I could grant him at least a little bit of grudging admiration.

Jim Borgman, no matter what you might think of him, is not afraid to face the tough issues – not afraid to come out with a controversial point of view – regardless of the consequences. For example, he's said it loud and clear, let the chips fall where they may, that yes, Japan *was* wrong for attacking Pearl Harbor.

But beyond this singular profile in courage, Jim day to day makes no attempt to cram a particular political philosophy down anyone's throat.

Professionally, he's a survivor. He survives editorial pages – right wing and left. No position on the spectrum of political thought lies immune. Just when you think he's tweaked the *Enquirer's* conservatism once too often, you rise the next morning to see some lefty cause fall prey to his killer pen. Yet there is no viciousness in it all. He attacks no one, save self-righteousness and pomposity – his only enemies.

He is creative, funny and incredibly perceptive. He can make a morning in Cincinnati. Perhaps we'll chuckle, or say "Yeah, boy is that right" – or maybe we'll even be angry. But if we are, the chances are it's because we don't always want to see what's there.

Well, if you can stomach people with talent (I can't), you are actually going to enjoy this book — indeed this man — whose vision is better than his sight.

Have a good time.

Jerry Springer

Where do you get your ideas?

The question I am most often asked as a cartoonist is "Where do you get your ideas?" I wish I knew. It seems to have something to do with staring at walls.

I start my day by reading, eventually choosing a topic about which I have an opinion. Then begins the search for an idea.

I usually sense that there are hundreds of good ideas out there if I can only glimpse them. If I am lucky, I receive a clue.

Contrary to popular opinion, cartoon ideas never come in the middle of the night.

My goal is to have several rough ideas by noon. On a rare day, ideas spring forth naturally and I must lock my door and ignore the phone so they can't escape.

Having settled on an idea, I spend the rest of my day trying to get the most out of it. Here are some ideas I am proud of. . .

The Road to Reaganomics

America elected Jimmy Carter President because he was an idealistic, proud-of-it outsider. Four years later, we turned him out because he had remained one.

For one thing, there were real-world problems…

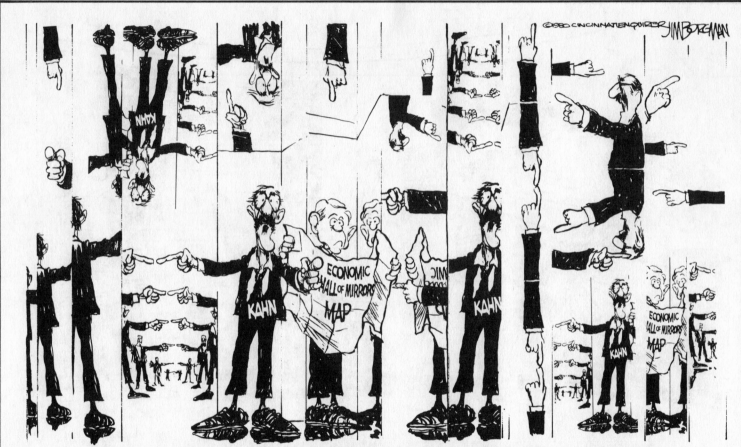

"THE WAY I SEE IT, MILLER, WE'VE BEEN HEADING THIS WAY, SO WE OUGHT TO START TURNING THAT WAY...."

17

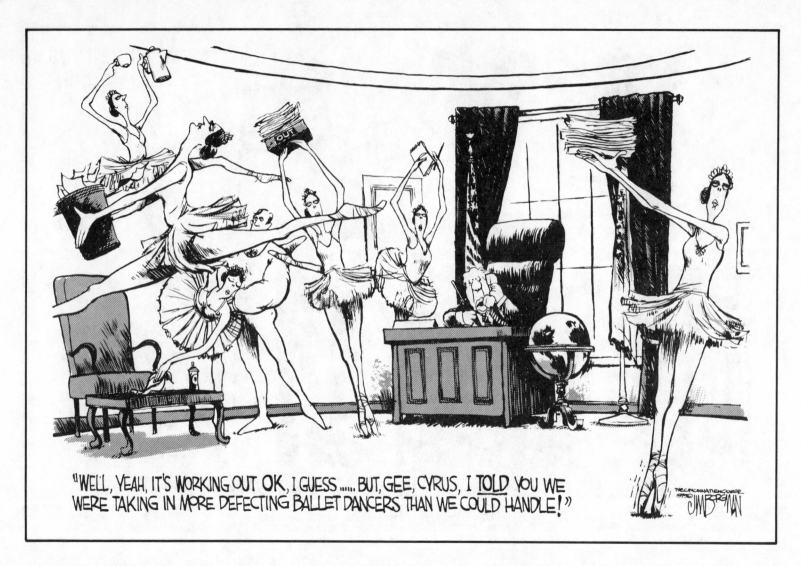

"WELL, YEAH, IT'S WORKING OUT OK, I GUESS ..... BUT, GEE, CYRUS, I TOLD YOU WE WERE TAKING IN MORE DEFECTING BALLET DANCERS THAN WE COULD HANDLE!"

There was also foreign-policy confusion – a rash of defections from the Russian Ballet...

...and a stalemate on the President's proudest and most promising effort.

The seizing of the American Embassy and its personnel in Iran symbolized the nation's growing sense of impotence in international affairs.

· AFTER ESCHER ·
©1980 THE CINCINNATI ENQUIRER   JIM BORGMAN

Impatient with the Ayatollah Khomeini's stalling, the President ordered the ill-fated rescue attempt of the hostages. Cyrus Vance had argued strongly against a military solution and left the administration soon after.

Ed Muskie was called in to tidy up the State Department.

Meanwhile, thousands flocked to see the Picasso retrospective at the Museum of Modern Art.

Carter made good his promise to get Ted Kennedy where it hurts – in the primaries.

Carter was more combative in his campaign than he had been in his presidency…

...although by then many of those caught in the economic squeeze had made up their minds about him.

"DON'T THOSE PEOPLE HAVE ANYTHING BETTER TO DO THAN THROW BOTTLES AND STAND AROUND IN UNEMPLOYMENT LINES?.... ER.... DON'T ANSWER THAT QUESTION........"

Throughout the GOP campaign, Jerry Ford waited by the telephone for a call that never came.

Reagan placated his feminist detractors by declaring that as President he would nominate a woman to the Supreme Court.

For the first time in years, there was a viable third-party candidate in John Anderson.

"....OR, OF COURSE, WE COULD JUST BAG THE WHOLE FLIPPIN' THING RIGHT HERE."

Khomeini considered releasing the hostages to help Carter defeat the more hawkish Reagan.

At least Brother Billy provided comic relief.

Carter diagnosed America's malaise as a lack of faith. As his presidency declined in the final year, the nation decided it had something to do with him.

BEDTIME FOR BONZO

Election Day, 1980.

Inauguration Day closed two chapters in Jimmy Carter's life – a humbling defeat and the crisis in Iran.

The New Look in Washington: All Right Wing

Ronald Reagan's Inauguration brought conservative fashions like top hats and morning coats back into style.

Reagan took immediate charge of the economy – what was left of it.

43

AND NOW, QUALIFYING AS THE WORLD'S SHORTEST HONEYMOON,...

Congress braced itself for battle.

"YES, I REPRESENT THE FEDERAL BUREAU OF BUREAUCRATIC PERPETUATION, AND ACCORDING TO OUR RECORDS YOU HAVE FAILED TO COMPLY WITH OUR REGULATIONS FOR THE HOLDING OF AN ECONOMIC JUDGMENT DAY, AND..."

Budget Director David Stockman slashed social programs with ruthless efficiency.

Solidarity emerged in Poland under the leadership of an electrician named Lech Walesa.

" ...AND THAT ABOUT WRAPS UP TODAY'S FOREIGN POLICY BRIEFING."

Alexander Haig, would-be vicar of foreign policy, was the administration's in-house Napoleon.

"THE IMAM SAYS HE MISSES THE HOSTAGES."

Ayatollah who?

A new generation of 18-year olds nonchalantly registered for a possible draft.

"...CONTINUING, THEN, ON OUR JOURNEY THROUGH TIME WE FIND OURSELVES BACK IN THE DAYS BEFORE DETENTE, BEFORE THE NEW DEAL AND BIG GOVERNMENT, BEFORE BUSING AND REGULATION, ... BACK IN A LITTLE COURTROOM IN A SLEEPY TENNESSEE TOWN...."

The '70's were gone but the '30's were back.

THE FOOL ON THE HILL

John Lennon dies of multiple handgun wounds.

JIMBORGMAN ©1981 CINCINNATI ENQUIRER

AN ARGUMENT AGAINST HANDGUN CONTROLS:

This argument is printed in the interest of fairness, with the belief that handgun owners should have as much opportunity to plead their case as handgun victims have to plead theirs.

Democratic leadership was stunned by Reagan's electoral mandate.

Black children everywhere had nightmares during a series of murders in Atlanta.

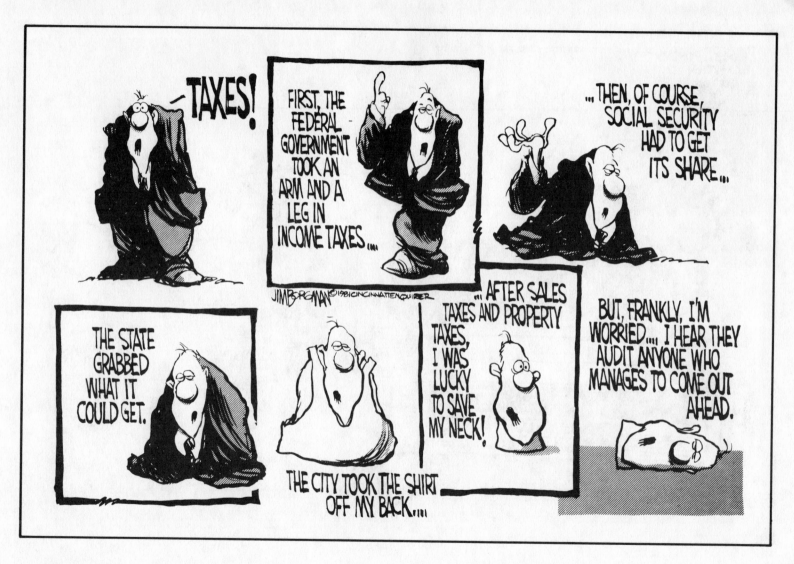

Tax time.

President Reagan and others are shot by a college-aged drifter trying to impress actress Jodie Foster.

" THE CRISIS? YES, MR. PRESIDENT, WE HAVE HIM UNDER CONTROL.....OH, YOU MEAN THE _OTHER_ CRISIS!"

In the ensuing confusion, Haig declared himself in charge, upstaging Vice-President Bush and permanently alienating Reagan's staff.

The threat of Soviet intervention in Poland loomed over most of the year in which...

…Russia had problems of its own.

"I LOOK FORWARD TO THE DAY WHEN WE'RE CIVILIZED AND WE DON'T HAVE TO SPEND HALF OUR BUDGET ON DEFENSE..."

SHUTTLE DIPLOMACY

The earth's first true spaceship, the shuttle, reshaped our understanding of the outer limits.

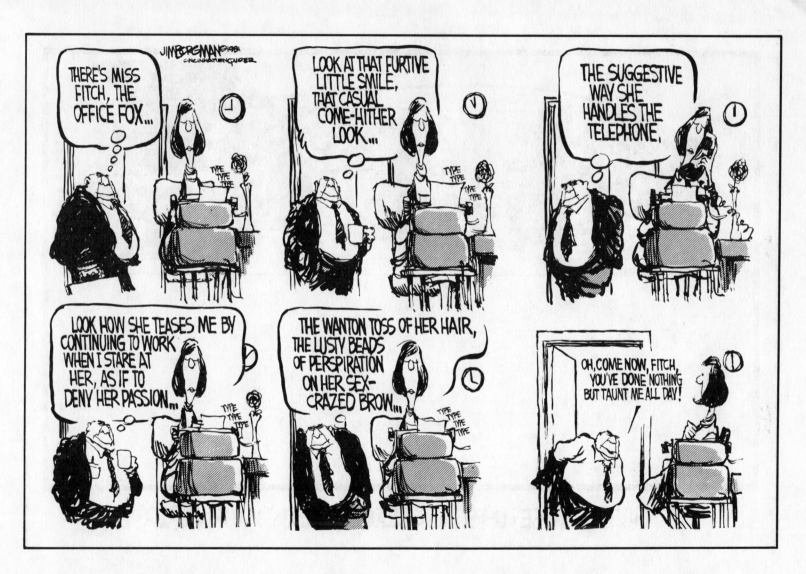

Phyllis Schlafly, anti-ERA spokesperson, took the curious position that working women had themselves to blame for sexual harassment in the office.

WHICH OF THESE POSES THE GREATER THREAT TO YOUR WORLD?

Pope John Paul II was the third prominent shooting victim within half a year, again proving that a dollar's worth of lead can change our world faster than a billion dollars' worth of bombs.

"OK, I'M ALEXANDER HAIG AND I'M IN CHARGE NOW..."

"I DUNNO, I THINK THE WEST WAS MORE ROMANTIC BEFORE THEY PAVED IT"

Charged with protecting the nation's resources, Secretary of Interior James Watt was like a wolf guarding sheep.

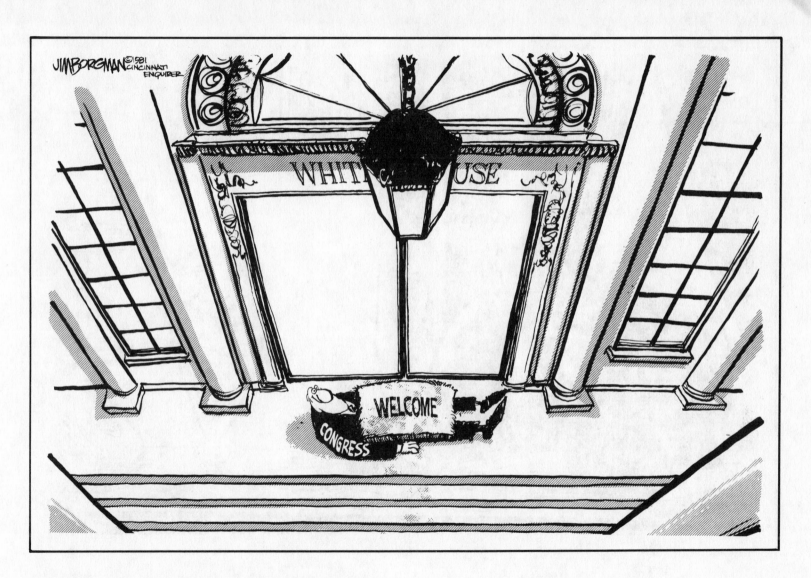

Congress was still adjusting to its role in Reagan's plan.

"ALL RIGHT THEN, DON'T PART!"

GAS LINES – 1981

America wallowed in the Arab oil glut...

...but continued to take a beating from the Japanese auto industry.

"V.A. Declares Victory in Vietnam Fiasco; Pulls Out."

"REMIND ME NOT TO ORDER THE FRUIT COCKTAIL AGAIN...."

The Year of the Medfly.

"WELL, AT LEAST IT'LL BE CHEAPER THAN IF HE'D HIRED A MAN..."

Reagan kept his promise and nominated a woman, Sandra Day O'Connor, to the Supreme Court...

...an inquisition by conservatives followed.

"CONGRATULATIONS, STOCKMAN... WE FINALLY GOT THE FEDERAL GOVERNMENT DOWN TO THE SIZE WE WANTED!"

Is Amy's tree house gone too?

"NOW WE'VE DONE IT! WE WENT AND TOLD A BUNCH OF JAMES WATT STORIES AND NOW WE'LL BE AWAKE ALL NIGHT!"

Where's Marlin Perkins when you really need him?

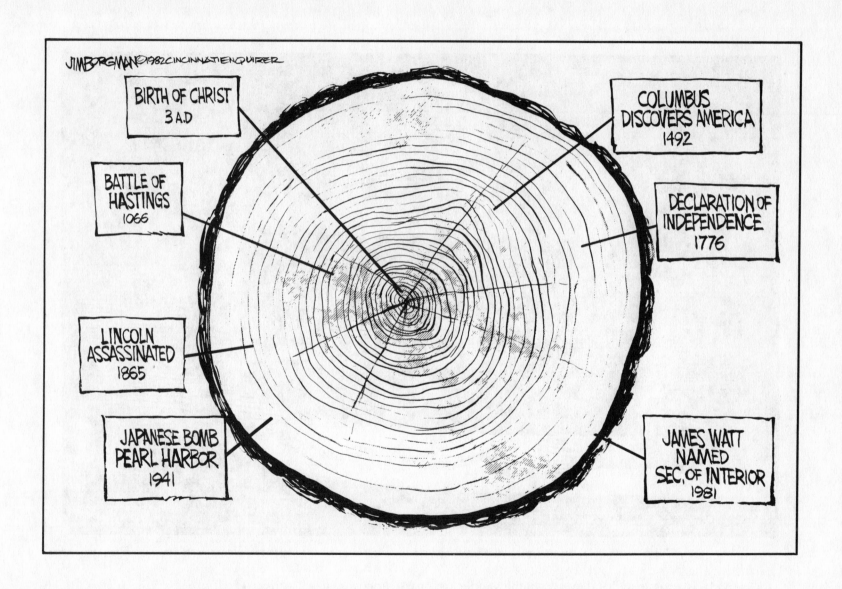

JIMBORGMAN ©1982 CINCINNATI ENQUIRER

BIRTH OF CHRIST
3 A.D

COLUMBUS
DISCOVERS AMERICA
1492

BATTLE OF
HASTINGS
1066

DECLARATION OF
INDEPENDENCE
1776

LINCOLN
ASSASSINATED
1865

JAPANESE BOMB
PEARL HARBOR
1941

JAMES WATT
NAMED
SEC. OF INTERIOR
1981

Anwar Sadat is assassinated and overnight the Middle East peace process begins to unravel.

Three former U.S. Presidents represented America at Sadat's funeral.

In a bizarre story, Lee Harvey Oswald's widow allowed her husband's body to be exhumed to end speculation by assassination theorists.

At the Cancun Summit on world economics, President Reagan insisted that God helps those who help themselves.

"IT'S CALLED SUPPLY-SIDE ECONOMICS....WE SUPPLY OUR SIDE AND YOU SUPPLY YOUR SIDE."

In an *Atlantic Monthly* article, David Stockman admitted his own doubts about Reaganomics...

...and characterized supply siders as Greeks bearing gifts.

" ' WHERE'S YOUR FAITH?' HE KEPT SAYING. 'TRUST MY REAGANOMICS!' HE SAID........
AND THEN HE DRIFTED OUT OF EARSHOT. "

There is a dangerous substance sweeping across America. It can be found in every elementary school, high school and college. Your children have probably tried it. Your neighbor may use it regularly. This menace, with its mind-altering effects, may threaten many of the values your community stands for. Americans everywhere are stamping it out before it changes their lives forever. Won't you help?

BOOKS.
If you find one, burn it.

Reactionaries rode in on the coattails of the conservative trend.

By December 1981, Solidarity had made its point all too well...

...and martial law was imposed.

"ONCE I GET A GOOD ROLLBACK STARTED, I JUST CAN'T HELP MYSELF!"

When the President proposed tax breaks for racially segregated schools, nearly everyone objected. The measure was quickly withdrawn.

Dan Rather recaptured Cronkite fans with cashmere.

John Belushi.

The Golden Years.

"RELAX, SAM ....DON'T YOU REMEMBER THAT CHANGING COURSE WAS CARTER'S BIG MISTAKE?"

Reagan asked America to hang in there, reasoning that the recession had to hurt before it helped.

Despite American match-making, El Salvador's romance with democracy remained stormy.

Argentina and Britain traded insults and then artillery fire over a few hundred square miles of real estate called the Falklands.

"SILLY ME.... AND I DIDN'T BELIEVE NUCLEAR WAR WAS SURVIVABLE!"

Talk about nuclear war became increasingly casual.

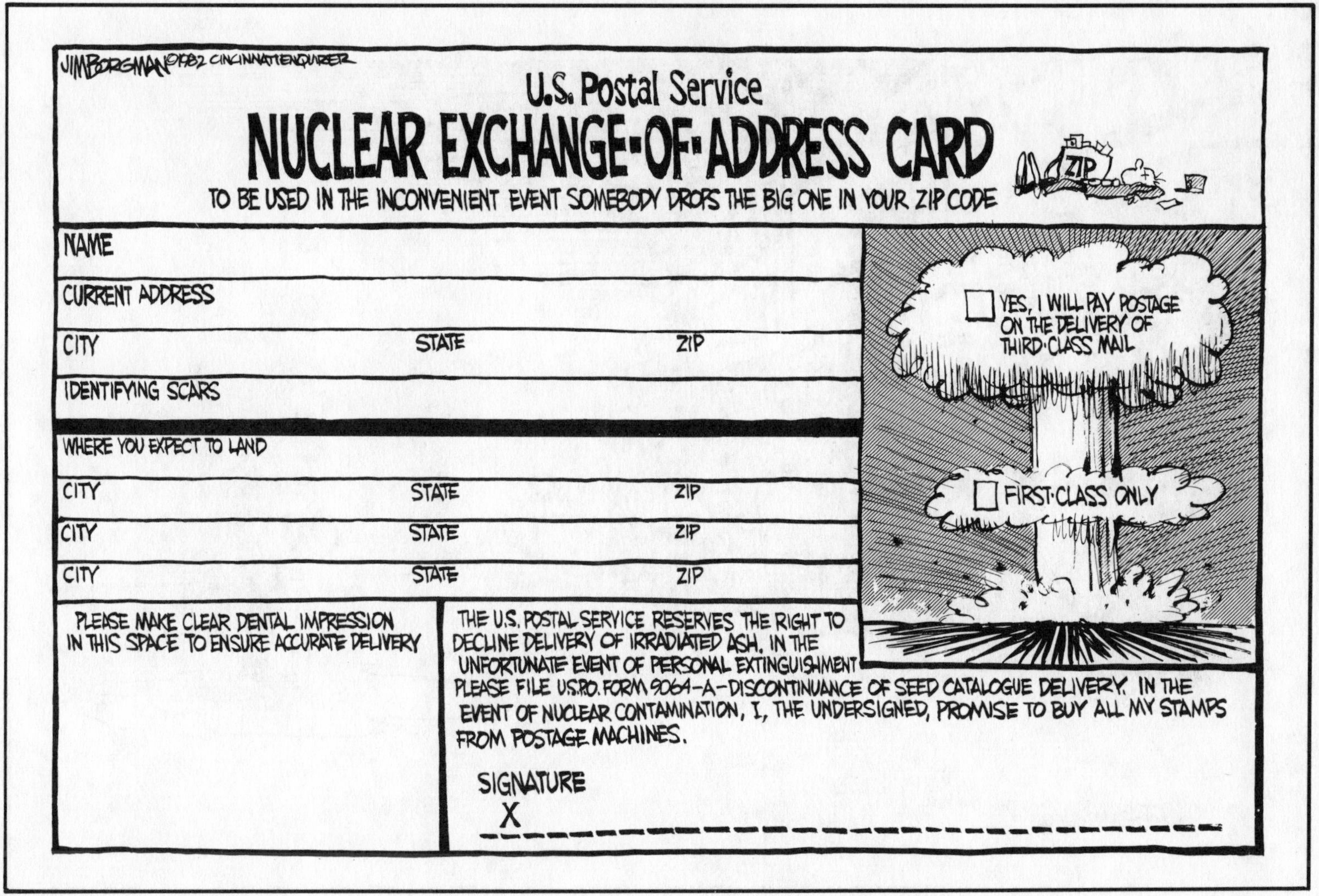
JIMBORGMAN©1982 CINCINNATI ENQUIRER
U.S. Postal Service
NUCLEAR EXCHANGE-OF-ADDRESS CARD
TO BE USED IN THE INCONVENIENT EVENT SOMEBODY DROPS THE BIG ONE IN YOUR ZIP CODE
ZIP
NAME
CURRENT ADDRESS
CITY STATE ZIP
IDENTIFYING SCARS
WHERE YOU EXPECT TO LAND
CITY STATE ZIP
CITY STATE ZIP
CITY STATE ZIP
YES, I WILL PAY POSTAGE ON THE DELIVERY OF THIRD-CLASS MAIL
FIRST-CLASS ONLY
PLEASE MAKE CLEAR DENTAL IMPRESSION IN THIS SPACE TO ENSURE ACCURATE DELIVERY
THE U.S. POSTAL SERVICE RESERVES THE RIGHT TO DECLINE DELIVERY OF IRRADIATED ASH. IN THE UNFORTUNATE EVENT OF PERSONAL EXTINGUISHMENT PLEASE FILE U.S.P.O. FORM 9064-A-DISCONTINUANCE OF SEED CATALOGUE DELIVERY. IN THE EVENT OF NUCLEAR CONTAMINATION, I, THE UNDERSIGNED, PROMISE TO BUY ALL MY STAMPS FROM POSTAGE MACHINES.
SIGNATURE
X

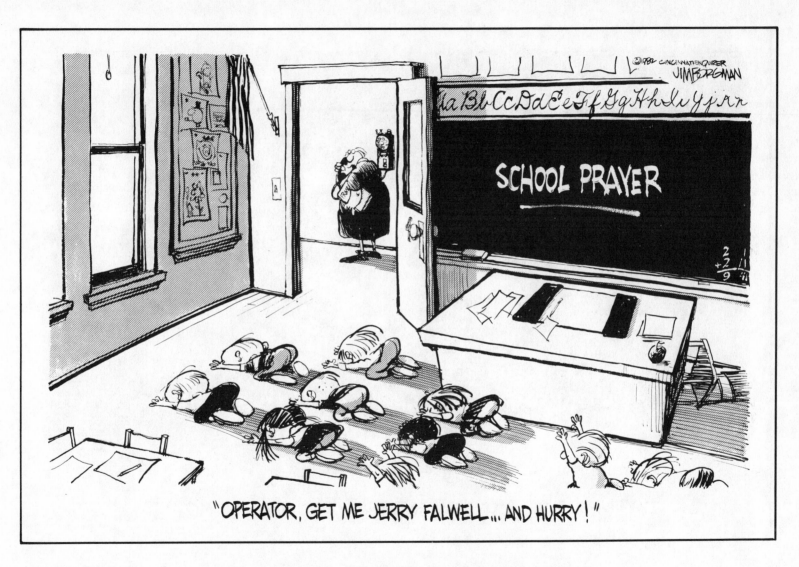

The Moral Majority continued to do unto others as they would prefer others not do unto them.

UNVEILING OF THE BOLD NEW ALTERNATIVE TO REAGANOMICS

Democratic leadership came up with its own budget package.

IF THERE'S ONE THING THAT MAKES ME REALLY ANGRY IT'S THE WAY THESE DEMOCRATS ARE SCARING OUR OLDER AMERICANS ON THE SOCIAL SECURITY ISSUE.

THEY'RE FRIGHTENING A LOT OF POOR, DEFENSELESS PEOPLE BY TELLING THEM HOW MUCH OUR $40 BILLION CUTS ARE GOING TO HURT THEM.

CALL ME A SOFTIE, BUT I JUST DON'T THINK IT'S RIGHT TO GO AROUND TERROR-IZING OLD PEOPLE.

THERE THEY ARE, CRITICIZING CUTS THEY HAD NOTHING TO DO WITH AND THEY DON'T EVEN SUPPORT!

THAT REMINDS ME OF A STORY..... SEEMS THERE WAS THIS FELLA HAD TWO CHICKENS. ONE SAYS TO THE OTHER, "WHICH CAME FIRST, THE OMELET OR THE EGG?" THE OTHER ONE SAYS, "THAT'S WHY I CROSSED THE ROAD!"

WELL, THAT'S JUST LIKE THE DEMOCRATS. NOW I DON'T WANT TO BEAT A DEAD BUSH, BUT LET ME JUST SAY—

CINCINNATI ENQUIRER
JIM BORGMAN 1982

MATH BY DAVID STOCKMAN, LOGIC BY RONALD REAGAN

"PRAISE THE LORD! A TORMENTED SOUL!"

SUCH A CUTE LITTLE WAR

The U.S. tried to remain neutral about the Falklands where an argument between two of our allies turned into a full-scale war.

Eventually, the U.S. got tough with Argentina about its aggression, a stance Reagan had trouble asserting as Israel invaded Lebanon.

A European youth movement challenged the superpowers on nuclear armament.

"OH, SURE, YOU'LL ALWAYS HAVE YOUR FRINGE ELEMENT..."

"LOOK, ALL I KNOW IS, ONE DAY THE COURT RULED WE HAVE TO ACCEPT ILLEGAL ALIENS IN OUR SCHOOLS, AND THE NEXT DAY HE ENROLLED."

E.T. waddled into our hearts in the summer of '82…

...as did young Prince William.

The ERA died a fitful death though polls showed that a great majority of Americans still supported it.

"PARDON ME A MOMENT, MR. HINCKLEY....I BELIEVE WE HAVE AN EMERGENCY CASE."

John Hinckley was found innocent by reason of insanity in the shooting of the President.

Alexander Haig left the State Department in a huff and George Shultz stepped in.

THE WAR THAT WON'T END

Ten years had passed since America's withdrawal from Southeast Asia.

What is this man doing?

At the first sign of profits, Chrysler's long-suffering workers demanded theirs.

NOAH RECEIVES A SIGN

Reagan promised rainbows but none could be seen here...

WHEN I WAS HOMELESS YOU GAVE ME YOUR BOMBS

JIM BORGMAN
©1982 CINCINNATTENQUIRER

...or in the Middle East where Israeli bombs destroyed Lebanese homes and Palestinians still searched for theirs.

But there is always hope as the world passes into the hands of new generations...

...a little worse for wear.

Welcome to Cinsanity, Ohio

Cincinnati is a town in which there is no lack of leadership.

We enjoy the simple pleasures of life.

For the time being, Cincinnati is a safe place to live…

...unless you happen to be a school tax levy...

...or need to get to the west side for some reason.

Visitors to Cincy often ask how we keep our cost of living down...

...and what makes the east side different from the west.

We are proud to tell newcomers of major exhibits at our art museum...

...and of our recently refurbished public library.

"HEY, ARE YOU SURE THIS IS HOW THEY GOT STARTED IN NEW YORK?"

Cincinnati has a great deal of stature among other cities, enough to command the interest of national organizations.

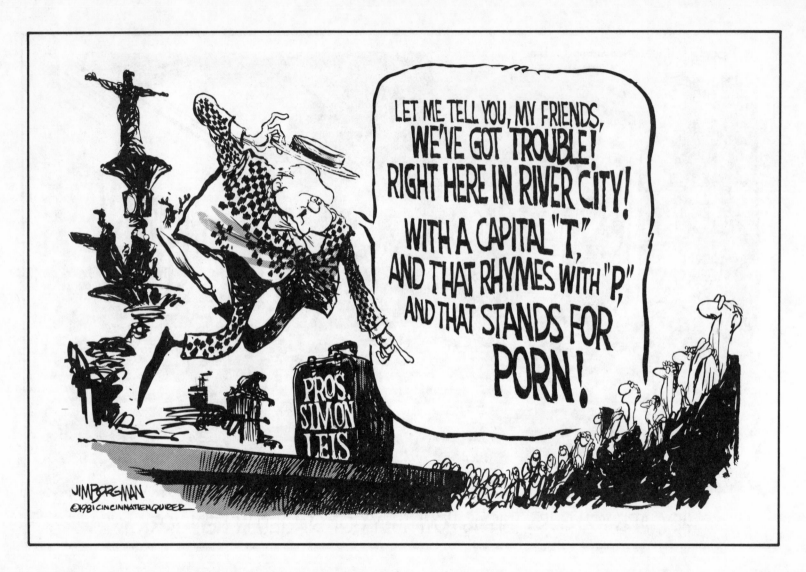

However, few people believe we need more guardian angels.

"OH, FOR PETE'S SAKE, KEN ....WHY CAN'T YOU JUST PICK A PARTY LIKE EVERYBODY ELSE?!"

Life in Cin City is anything but dull. Former Mayor Ken Blackwell made a major theatrical production of switching parties.

Mayor Mann rode elephants and christened bowling alleys.

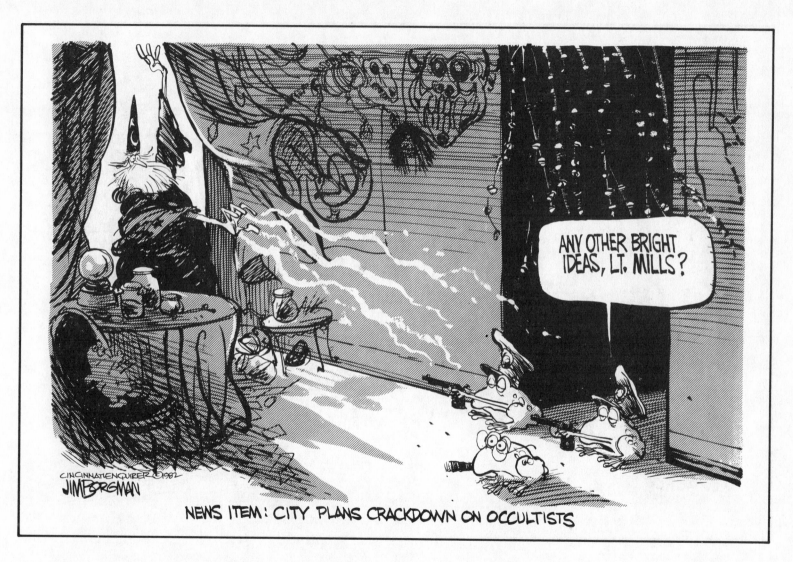

NEWS ITEM: CITY PLANS CRACKDOWN ON OCCULTISTS

In other news, the city worried about its shrinking police force.

Outlying townships sized up the city's share of tax revenue and tried to muscle some of it back.

"I PREFER THE LITTLE ONES."

County Prosecutor Simon Leis felt that a local gay broadcast violated community standards more than alleged campaign improprieties in county government.

Citing union demands, Kahn's threatened to take its wieners elsewhere in the world.

It took a legal battle to situate a neighborhood home for the mentally retarded.

For many years, Ohio was fortunate to have a man of great vision for governor.

As the Rhodes dynasty faded, a few new faces popped up in the gubernatorial race.

At least one bright, young politician was aware that Ohio historically has been a springboard for better things.

Jerry Springer might have won the Democratic slot if an Election Day monsoon had hit Cuyahoga instead of Hamilton County.

Another favorite son failed upstate.

We Cincinnatians are very chauvinistic about our sports teams. We gripe privately about how they are doing but defend them with fierce optimism to outsiders.

"I ALWAYS SAID IT WOULD BE A COLD DAY DOWN HERE WHEN THE BENGALS REACHED THE SUPER BOWL!"

However, even we were surprised when the Bengals donned new uniforms and clawed their way to the top of the NFL in 1981.

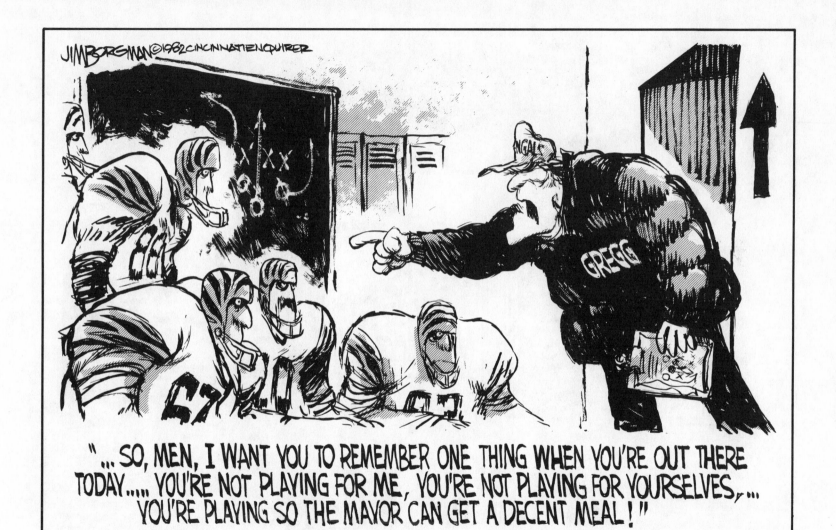

Mayor Feinstein of San Francisco gambled groceries with Mayor Mann over the Super Bowl match. In the end, it was Mann who had to fork over the stakes.

Baseball lost a bit of its innocence after the strike of '81. Hero worship diminished...

...probably because most of our heroes had been traded.

In a last ditch effort to save the '82 season, Reds management impeached John McNamara and called in a proven leader.

Some people say that Cincinnatians take sports too seriously. However, we feel that it is the kind of good, clean fun that keeps families together.

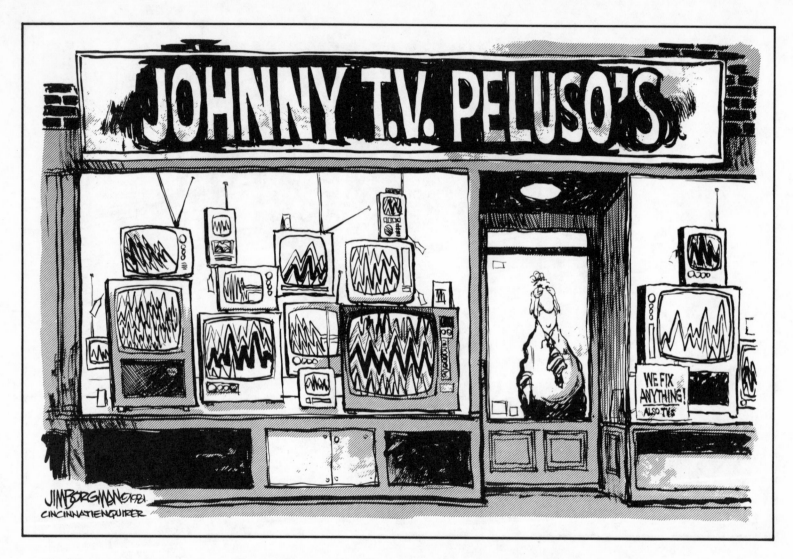

Cincinnati said goodbye to some familiar faces in the last year, including Newport's leading media celebrity...

...best friend to the city's most published cockroach...

...and a man who, for 23 years, never saw the late news in his own living room.

"I'LL BET DICK WAGNER HAD SOMETHING TO DO WITH THIS!"

For some people, Cincinnati is just one stop on the way to better things. It makes us feel sad and dejected but then…

"THEY FORGOT TO CONSIDER ONE THING, JOHNSON — WHO WANTS TO GO TO CLEVELAND FAST?"

...there's always Cleveland to dump on.